by Ellen Lawrence

Consultants:

Suzy Gazlay, MA
Recipient, Presidential Award for Excellence in Science Teaching

Kimberly Brenneman, PhD
National Institute for Early Education Research, Rutgers University, New Brunswick, New Jersey

BEARPORT PUBLISHING

New York, New York

Credits

Cover, © Konkolas/Shutterstock and © iwana/Shutterstock; 3, © CoraMax/Shutterstock and © Ilin Sergey/Shutterstock; 4–5, © 2happy/Shutterstock, © Blend Images/Shutterstock, © lapetitelumiere/Shutterstock, © One02/Shutterstock, © CoraMax/Shutterstock, © ancroft/Shutterstock, © Dennis Nata/Shutterstock, © Mi. Ti./Shutterstock, © Andrey Arkusha/Shutterstock, © Photosync/Shutterstock, © Gilmanshin/Shutterstock, and © Leah Anne-Thompson/Shutterstock; 6–7, © CoraMax/Shutterstock, © Picsfive/Shutterstock, © Spectral Design/Shutterstock, and © 3Dprofi/Shutterstock; 8–9, © CoraMax/Shutterstock and © Sergieiev/Shutterstock; 10–11, © CoraMax/Shutterstock, © Arena Creative/Shutterstock, © Kesu/Shutterstock, © Ruby Tuesday Books, and © Andrey Kuzmin/Shutterstock; 12–13, © CoraMax/Shutterstock, © Givaga/Shutterstock, © Imageman/Shutterstock, © Peredniankina/Shutterstock, © Abel Turmik/Shutterstock, and © Ruby Tuesday Books; 14–15, © CoraMax/Shutterstock, © Ruby Tuesday Books, © bayberry/Shutterstock, and © Scruggelgreen/Shutterstock; 16–17, © CoraMax/Shutterstock, © Ruby Tuesday Books, and © Topseller/Shutterstock; 18–19, © CoraMax/Shutterstock, © iStockphoto, © cenap refik ongan/Shutterstock, © Ruby Tuesday Books, © Ilona Baha/Shutterstock, and © Danny Smythe/Shutterstock; 20–21, © CoraMax/Shutterstock, © Ruby Tuesday Books, and © Sergieiev/Shutterstock; 22, © iStockphoto, © Kesu/Shutterstock, © Cultura Limited/Superstock, © veryan dale/Alamy, © Ron Chapple/Alamy, and © H. Eisenbeiss/FLPA; 23, © Subbotina Anna/Shutterstock, © Zurijeta/Shutterstock, © Severe/Shutterstock, and © jaroslava V/Shutterstock.

Publisher: Kenn Goin
Editorial Director: Adam Siegel
Creative Director: Spencer Brinker
Design: Emma Randall
Photo Researcher: Ruby Tuesday Books Ltd.

Library of Congress Cataloging-in-Publication Data in process at time of publication (2013)
Library of Congress Control Number: 2012046342
ISBN-13: 978-1-61772-736-8 (library binding)

For more information, write to Bearport Publishing Company, Inc., 45 West 21st Street, Suite 3B, New York, NY 10010. Printed in the United States of America.

10 9 8 7 6 5 4 3 2 1

Contents

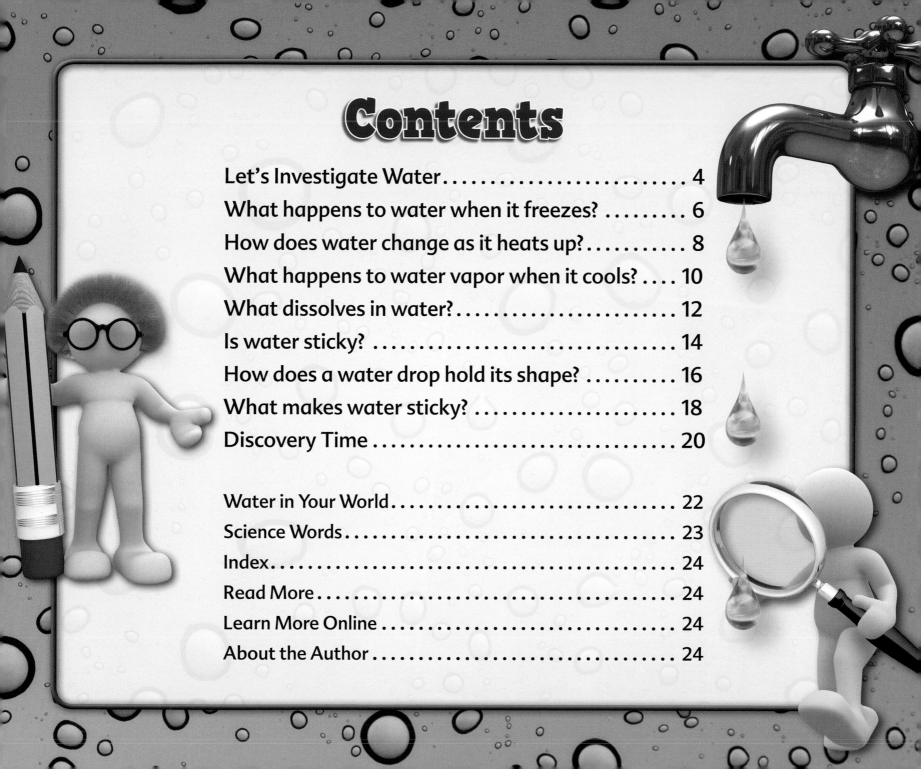

Let's Investigate Water

You drink it, bathe in it, and probably like to swim and splash in it. You see and use water every day, but now it's time to look at this amazing **liquid** like a scientist. Inside this book are lots of fun experiments and cool facts about water. So grab a notebook, and let's start investigating!

Check It Out!

Like all liquids, water doesn't have a shape. Instead, it **flows** and takes the shape of whatever container it's in. Let's investigate to see how.

- Find some plastic containers in your home that are different shapes.

- Fill a measuring cup with water and pour it into the different containers.

- Observe how the water flows and becomes different shapes.

- Describe the shapes or draw them in your notebook.

- Now, suck some water through a straw to see how water can take on a long and thin or curly shape!

What happens to water when it freezes?

Most of the time, water is a liquid. For example, we see waves in the ocean, raindrops in the sky, or water in a bathtub. Water isn't always in its liquid form, though. When the air **temperature** drops to 32°F (0°C), water freezes and is no longer a liquid. What does it become? Let's investigate to find out.

You will need:

- A black marker
- A clear plastic cup
- Water
- A freezer
- A notebook and pencil

1 Make a black line about halfway up on the side of a plastic cup.

2 Pour water into the cup up to the black line.

3 Place the cup in a freezer.

▶ **What do you think will happen to the water?**

Write down your **predictions** in your notebook.

 4 After three hours, take the cup out of the freezer.

▶ **How has the water changed?**

▶ **Why did the water change?**

▶ **When the water was a liquid, it filled up the cup all the way to the black line. What do you observe about the water now?**

Record what happened in your notebook.

▶ Do your predictions match what happened?

 5 Leave the cup on a countertop and observe how the frozen water changes.

(To learn more about this investigation and find the answers to the questions, see pages 20–21.)

How does water change as it heats up?

Water isn't always a liquid or a **solid**. It can take another form, too. When liquid water heats up, it changes into an invisible **gas** called **water vapor**. There is water vapor floating in the air all around us—but we can't see it. So how can we tell it's there? Let's investigate by watching what happens to a puddle of water as it heats up.

You will need:

- A cup of water
- A hard surface, such as a sidewalk or blacktop
- A notebook and pencil
- Colored chalk

1 On a warm day, go outside and pour some water onto a hard surface to make a puddle.

▶ **What do you think will happen to the water?**

Write down your predictions in your notebook.

Use colored chalk to draw an outline around the edges of the puddle.

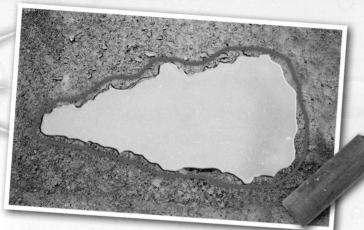

 Check the water every ten minutes for one hour and draw a new outline around it each time.

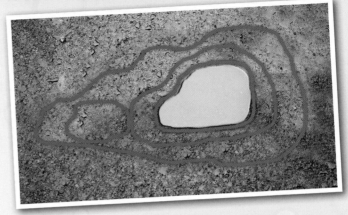

▶ What do you think happened to the puddle?

▶ Where do you think the water is now?

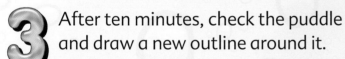 After ten minutes, check the puddle and draw a new outline around it.

▶ What do you observe happening to the water?

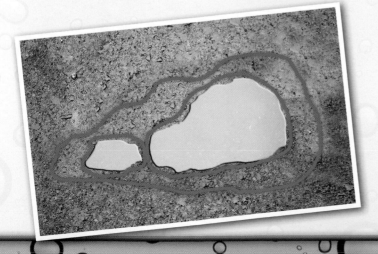

In your notebook, record how the puddle changed.

▶ Do your predictions match what happened to the water?

(To learn more about this investigation and find the answers to the questions, see pages 20–21.)

What happens to water vapor when it cools?

When water vapor in the air cools, it changes back into liquid water. You can't see water vapor in the air. However, if the vapor touches something cold, it becomes water that you can see. Let's investigate!

You will need:

- Some ice cubes
- Two glasses
- A notebook and pencil

1 Place some ice cubes in a glass.

2 Stand the glass on a countertop. Then place an empty glass on the countertop about 12 inches (30 cm) from the first glass.

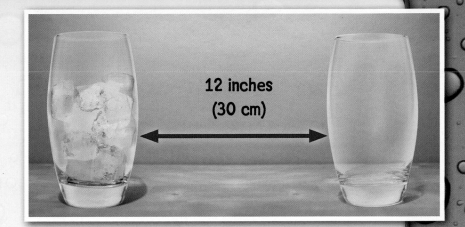

12 inches (30 cm)

3 After 15 minutes, look closely at the glasses.

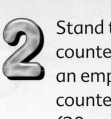

In your notebook, record what you see on the outside of the glass with ice cubes.

▶ What do you think has happened?

Now record in your notebook what you see on the outside of the second glass.

▶ Why do you think it's different from the glass filled with ice cubes?

(To learn more about this investigation and find the answers to the questions, see pages 20-21.)

11

What dissolves in water?

When water is in its liquid form, it's possible to mix it with other **substances**. Sometimes, these substances seem to disappear. That's because they have **dissolved**. The substances are still in the water, we just can't see them. Let's investigate what substances dissolve in water.

You will need:

- Salt, sugar, pepper, and sand
- A notebook and pencil
- Four clean, clear plastic cups
- Water
- Four teaspoons

1 Look closely at some salt, sugar, pepper, and sand.

▶ **What do you think will happen when you mix each of these substances with water?**

▶ **Will the substance:**
  - **float in the water?**
  - **sink to the bottom of the cup?**
  - **dissolve in the water?**

Write your predictions in your notebook.

salt

sugar

sand

pepper

12

Fill four clear plastic cups with water.

 Stir a teaspoon of salt into one cup of water.

▶ **Can you still see the salt?**

▶ **What is happening to the salt?**

In your notebook, record what you observe.

 Repeat the same experiment with the sugar, pepper, and then sand. Use a clean teaspoon and a different cup of water for each substance.

▶ **Do the substances float, sink, or dissolve?**

▶ **Can you still see them in the water?**

sand

In your notebook, write down what happened in each experiment.

▶ **Do your predictions match what happened?**

(To learn more about this investigation and find the answers to the questions, see pages 20–21.)

Is water sticky?

You can't use water to glue things together, but water is sticky in its own special way. If two drops of water touch, they will clump together to form a bigger drop. This special stickiness is called **cohesion**. Let's investigate water's stickiness.

1 Place a penny on a table or countertop.

2 Collect some water in an eyedropper and carefully squeeze one drop of water onto the penny.

Look carefully at the water drop.

▶ How would you describe it?

Draw the shape of the drop in your notebook.

You will need:

- A penny
- A cup of water
- An eyedropper
- A notebook and pencil

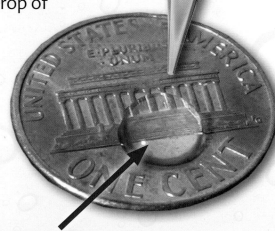

one drop

Now carefully add a second drop of water to the penny.

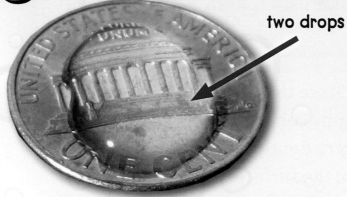

two drops

▶ **What do the drops of water do?**

▶ **How many drops of water do you think will fit on the penny?**

Write your prediction in your notebook.

Continue to carefully add water drops to the penny. Record the number of drops in your notebook using tally marks like this.

▶ **What are the drops of water doing now?**

In your notebook, draw the shape of the water on the penny.

‖‖‖ ‖‖‖ ‖‖

Keep adding water drops until the water spills off the penny.

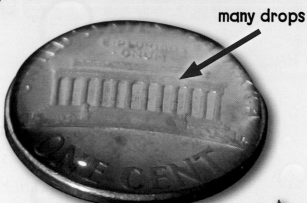

many drops

▶ **How many drops did you fit on the penny?**

▶ **Did you fit more or fewer drops than you predicted?**

▶ **Why do you think so many drops of water could fit on the penny?**

(To learn more about this investigation and find the answers to the questions, see pages 20–21.)

How does a water drop hold its shape?

If you look closely at a water drop, you'll see that it has a rounded surface. The drop is being held together by cohesion. The water on the outside of the drop is sticking extra tightly to the rest of the water. This pulling together of water on the surface of the drop is called **surface tension**. Try this experiment to see how surface tension keeps water from spilling out of a glass.

1 Carefully fill a glass to the very top with water.

You will need:

- A glass
- A pitcher of water
- 100 pennies
- A notebook and pencil

Gently drop a penny into the glass.

▶ **Did the water spill out?**

▶ **How many pennies do you think you can drop into the glass before the water spills over?**

Record your prediction in your notebook.

 Gently drop pennies into the water one at a time. Record the number of pennies in your notebook using tally marks.

 Look closely at the top of the glass from the side.

Describe what the water is doing.

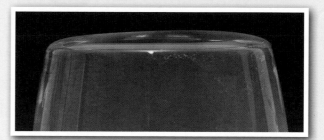

 Keep adding pennies and watch the water until it spills out of the glass.

▶ **How many pennies did you drop in the glass?**

▶ **Did more or fewer pennies fit in the glass than you predicted?**

▶ **What do you think stopped the water from spilling out of the glass sooner?**

(To learn more about this investigation and find the answers to the questions, see pages 20–21.)

What makes water sticky?

Water drops don't stick only to each other, they also stick to other things. For example, have you noticed that when you step out of the bath or shower, there are water droplets on your skin? The water is clinging, or sticking, to your skin. When water sticks to a surface it's called **adhesion**. Try this experiment to see how adhesion helps water to move from one cup to another.

You will need:

- A piece of string about ten inches (25 cm) long
- A pitcher of water
- Duct tape
- Two plastic cups
- A dish towel
- A notebook and pencil

1 Soak a string in water for about one minute.

2 Using two small pieces of duct tape, fasten the ends of the string to the inside rim of each cup.

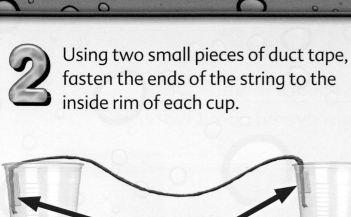

string taped
inside cups

cup A

cup B

3 Place a dish towel on a countertop and stand the cups on it. Fill cup B halfway with water.

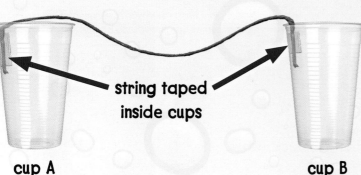

cup A   cup B

4 Lift up cup B. With your other hand, hold cup A steady on the countertop.

5 Gently tip cup B so the water starts to flow slowly out of the cup.

cup B

The cups should be in these positions.

cup A

Observe what is happening to the water and record your findings in your notebook.

▶ How is it possible for the water to move from one cup to the other in this way?

(To learn more about this investigation and find the answers to the questions, see pages 20–21.)

19

Discovery Time

Investigating the world using science is fun!
Now, let's check out all the things we discovered about water.

What happens to water when it freezes?

When the cup of water was put in the freezer, it changed from a liquid to a solid—ice.

Pages 6-7

Solid water takes up more space than liquid water, so the ice rose up above the black line on the cup.

When the cup of ice warmed up, the ice melted and changed back into liquid water.

Unlike liquid water, ice is a solid and has a shape.

ice

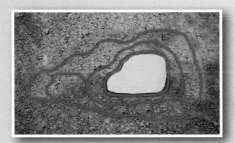

Pages 8-9

How does water change as it heats up?

When the water in the puddle heated up, the puddle got smaller and smaller.

This happened because the liquid water changed into water vapor and floated up into the air.

What happens to water vapor when it cools?

After 15 minutes on the countertop, the glass containing the ice cubes had water on the outside.

Pages 10-11

This happened because water vapor in the air cooled when it touched the cold glass and so it changed into liquid water.

water on outside of glass

The second glass stayed dry because it wasn't colder than the surrounding air. So, when vapor touched that glass, the vapor didn't cool down.

What dissolves in water?

salt sugar pepper sand

Sugar and salt dissolve in water.

These substances look as if they have disappeared.

You can check they are still there, though, by tasting the water. It will taste sweet or salty.

Pepper sinks or floats in the water, and you can still see it.

Sand sinks to the bottom of the cup of water, and you can still see it.

Pages 12-13

Is water sticky?

It's possible to fit lots of water drops on a penny.

This is because of cohesion.

The drops stick to each other and cling together to make one big drop.

Pages 14-15

How does a water drop hold its shape?

water bulge

The glass was completely filled with water, yet lots of pennies were able to fit in the glass without the water spilling over the top.

Did you see the water making a bulge at the top of the glass?

This happened because of surface tension. The water at the very top of the glass was sticking together extra tightly, so it did not spill out.

Pages 16-17

What makes water sticky?

The water flowed down the string into the empty cup.

The water did this because of cohesion and adhesion.

The water drops were sticking to each other (cohesion) and to the string (adhesion) and, as a result, didn't fall onto the counter.

Pages 18-19

21

Water in Your World

Water doesn't do exciting things only during scientific experiments. Check out the ways that you can see amazing water in action every day!

1. On a hot day, it's great to have a cool drink with ice cubes in it.

▶ **What happens to the ice as the drink gets warm?**

2. When you get out of the shower or swimming pool, your hair is wet. It soon dries, though.

▶ **Where did the water on your hair go?**

3. On a cold morning, have you noticed water on the inside of the windows in your home?

▶ **How did the water get there?**

4. When you're in a car or on the school bus and it rains, watch the raindrops trickle down the window.

▶ **What do you notice about the raindrops?**

5. You might see insects walking on the water in a pond.

▶ **How do you think they can do this?**

Answers: 1. The ice melts and becomes liquid water. 2. Water vapor in the air inside the house touched the cold glass and changed into liquid water. 3. Water vapor in the air touched the cold window and changed into liquid water. 4. The raindrops stick to the glass and sometimes join together to make bigger drops because of adhesion and cohesion. 5. The tiniest drops of water stick together extra tightly at the surface of a pond where the water meets the air. This is called surface tension. Some insects can walk on water because of surface tension. These insects are light and they have feet that are shaped to float on the surface without breaking the surface tension of the water.

Science Words

adhesion (ad-HEE-zhuhn) the sticking together of two different substances; for example, water sticking to glass

cohesion (koh-HEE-zhuhn) the sticking, or joining together, of a substance; for example, one water drop sticking to another water drop

dissolved (di-ZOLVD) became part of a liquid and seemed to disappear; for example, sugar mixing with and becoming part of liquid water

flows (FLOHZ) to move in a liquid form

gas (GASS) matter that floats in the air and is neither a liquid nor a solid; most gases, such as water vapor, are invisible

liquid (LIK-wid) matter that is neither a solid nor a gas; a liquid flows and changes its shape to fit whatever container it is placed in

predictions (pri-DIK-shuhns) guesses that something will happen in a certain way; they are often based on facts a person knows or something a person has observed

solid (SOL-id) matter that is neither a liquid nor a gas; a solid has a definite size and shape

substances (SUHB-stuhns-iz) materials or types of matter, often grouped as liquids, solids, or gases.

surface tension (SUR-fiss TEN-shuhn) the sticking, or pulling together, of the outside layer of a liquid, such as water, because of cohesion

temperature (TEM-pur-uh-chur) a measurement of how hot or cold something is

water vapor (WAW-tur VAY-pur) water that has changed into a gas; water vapor rises and spreads out through the air

Index

Read More

Hume, Desmond. *Earth's Water (Exploring Earth and Space).* New York: Rosen (2013).

Lawrence, Ellen. *What Is the Water Cycle? (Weather Wise).* New York: Bearport (2012).

Oxlade, Chris. *Water (How Does My Home Work?).* Chicago: Heinemann Library (2013).

Learn More Online

To learn more about water, visit
www.bearportpublishing.com/FundamentalExperiments

About the Author

Ellen Lawrence lives in the United Kingdom. Her favorite books to write are those about nature and animals. In fact, the first book Ellen bought for herself, when she was six years old, was the story of a gorilla named Patty Cake that was born in New York's Central Park Zoo.

24